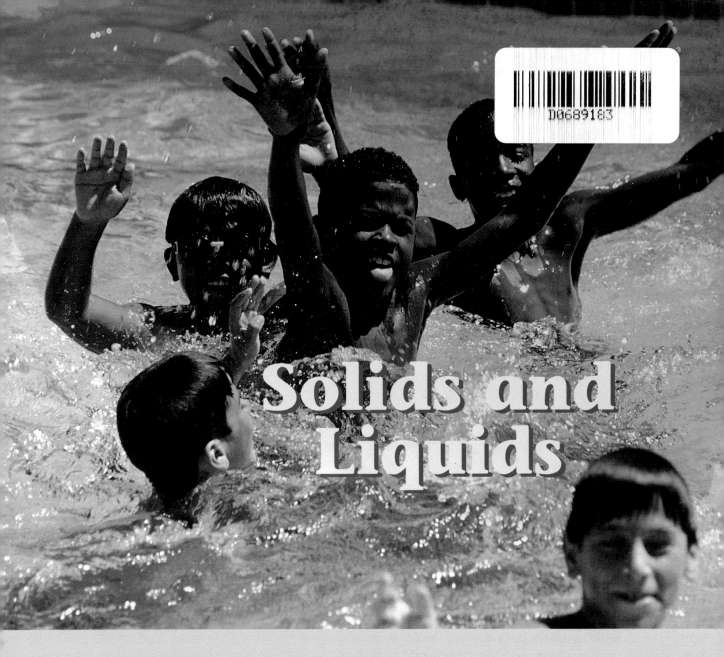

Solids and Liquids

Developed at
Lawrence Hall of Science
University of California at Berkeley

Published and Distributed by **Delta Education**

ISBN 1-58356-460-8

542-1272

6 7 8 9 10 SPC 06 05 04 03

Table of Contents

Everything Matters

The world is made up of many things.
Trees, bubbles, slides, and drinking
fountains are just some of them.
These things may all seem very
different. But in one way, they are all
the same. They are all matter. Matter
is anything that takes up space.

Matter can be divided
into three groups.
They are solids, liquids,
and gases.

A slide is a solid.

Flowing water is a liquid.

Bubbles are filled with air. Air is a gas.
How did the gas get into the bubble? What
happens if you touch a bubble?

We use solids and liquids all the time.
Every solid and liquid is different. So they
are useful in different ways.

Cement bricks are strong and
hard. They are just right for
building walls.

Wool is soft and flexible. It is
good for hats and scarves.

Water is easy to spray and splash.
It makes a hot summer day lots of fun!

Look around you for solids and liquids.
How will you use them today?

Solids and Liquids

What is the difference between solids and liquids? They have different properties. Properties describe how something looks or feels.

Shape and size are two properties of a solid. The shape and size don't change unless you do something to them. Solids can be rigid, like a bat. When something is rigid, you can't bend it.

Solids can be flexible, like a sweater. When something is flexible, you can bend it.

Some solids can be broken into pieces. Each piece has a different shape and takes up less space.

When you put the pieces back together, it has the same shape as before. It takes up the same space, too.

Solids can be very small, like sand.
You can pour sand out of a bucket.
But every grain of sand is a solid.

Liquids have properties, too. A liquid can be poured. It doesn't have its own shape. It takes the shape of the container that holds it.

A liquid has a different shape in each container.

Liquids can be foamy, bubbly, or transparent. They can be translucent or viscous.

Solids and liquids are all
around you. Can you find
the solids in each picture?
Can you find the liquids?

Solids to Liquids and Back Again

Solids can change to liquids,
and liquids can change to solids.

Butter is a solid. But if you heat the
butter, it melts. It becomes a liquid.

This hot, liquid chocolate turns solid
as it cools.

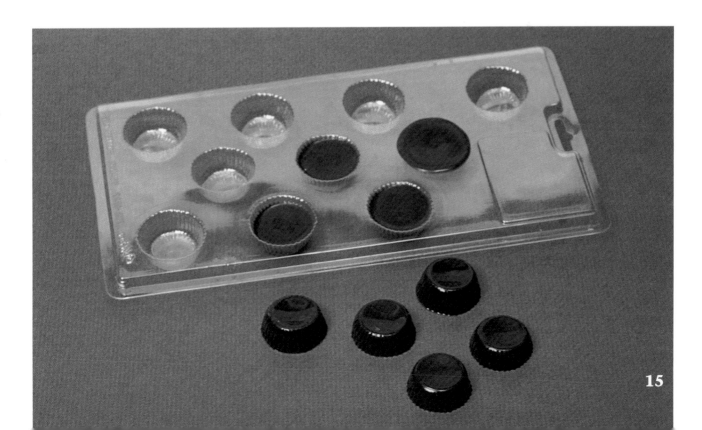

Liquid water can become a
solid if you freeze it. Ice!

If you take ice out of the
freezer, it melts. It becomes
a liquid again.

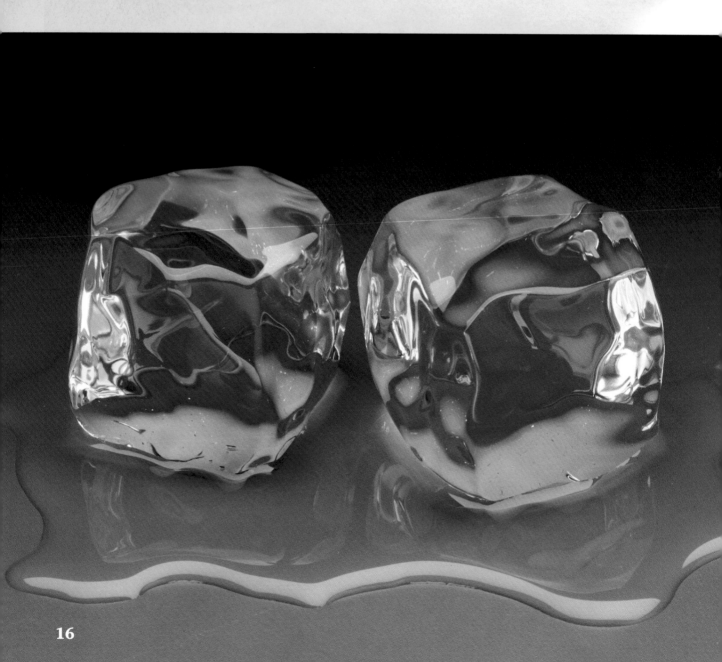

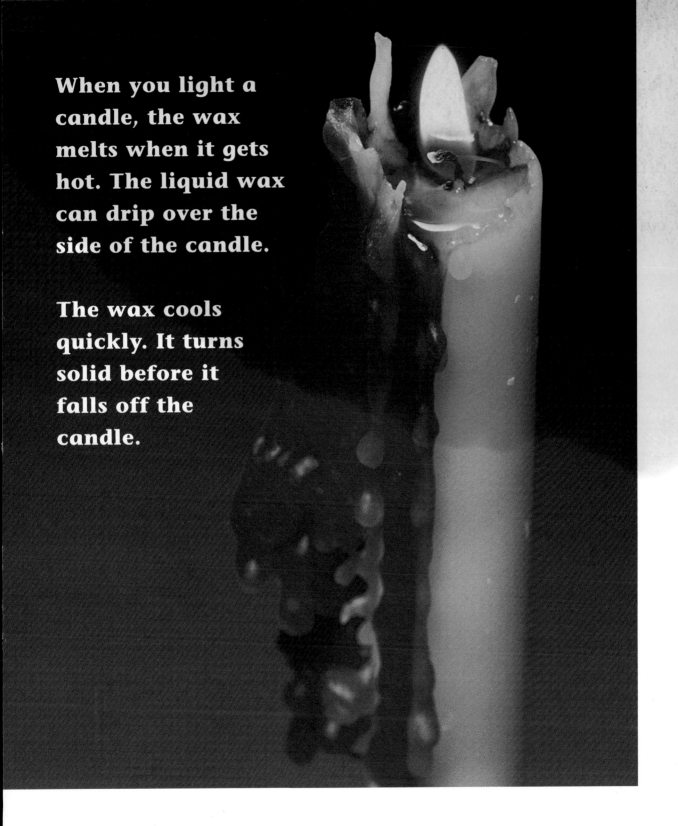

When you light a candle, the wax melts when it gets hot. The liquid wax can drip over the side of the candle.

The wax cools quickly. It turns solid before it falls off the candle.

What makes solids and liquids change?
Heating them up or cooling them down!

Mix It Up!

When you mix two or more things with different properties, you get a mixture.

What happens when you mix two solids?

What happens when you mix two liquids?

It depends. Sometimes the liquids mix together to make one new liquid.

Sometimes they don't mix. The two liquids form layers.

What happens when a solid is mixed
with a liquid?

Sometimes the solid seems to
disappear. It dissolves. The solid
breaks apart into tiny pieces. The
pieces are so small, you can't see them.

How do you know the solid is there? If you wait long enough, the liquid will evaporate. Then, you can see the solid again. But it might look different.

Solids and liquids are everywhere.
How do you use solids and liquids?

Try mixing them up. Try to
change them.

Think about what would happen
if there were no solids or liquids.
Nothing would be the same!

Glossary

Bubbly - describes a liquid that is full of bubbles.

Dissolve - when a solid is mixed with a liquid, and the solid breaks down into pieces so small they can't be seen in the liquid.

Foamy - describes a liquid that has a layer of bubbles on top.

Liquid - matter that flows freely. Water is one kind.

Matter - anything that takes up space.

Mixture - two or more materials stirred together.

Property - something you can observe. Size, color, and shape are properties.

Solid - matter that has a definite shape and always takes up the same amount of space.

Translucent - describes a liquid or solid that is clear enough to let light go through, but not transparent. A frosted window is translucent.

Transparent - describes a liquid or solid that you can see through. Water is transparent.

Viscous - describes a liquid that is thick and slow moving. Honey is viscous.